IMAGES
of America

HARTWOOD ACRES

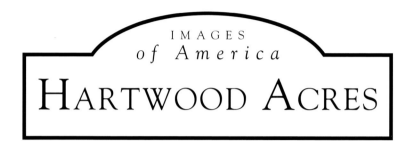

IMAGES
of America

HARTWOOD ACRES

Lisa Speranza

ARCADIA
PUBLISHING

Published by Arcadia Publishing
Charleston, South Carolina

Printed in the United States of America

Library of Congress Control Number: 2022937553

For all general information, please contact Arcadia Publishing:
Telephone 843-853-2070
Fax 843-853-0044
E-mail sales@arcadiapublishing.com
For customer service and orders:
Toll-Free 1-888-313-2665

Visit us on the Internet at www.arcadiapublishing.com

Dedicated to single parents everywhere who have persevered through adversity, risen above struggle, and who have loved more deeply than these words could ever capture

CONTENTS

ACKNOWLEDGMENTS

At the very heart of the home known as Hartwood was family. It is a word that can be defined in many measures. In one sense, it encompasses a couple, or parents and their children. It is therefore vitally important to first and foremost acknowledge that this project would not have been possible without the love and dedication that John and Mary Lawrence put into the family they raised here. They shared this home first together and then, with their children, adopted in the late 1930s / early 1940s. For the Lawrences, family extended beyond their own to include the numerous other attendants of the home. These individuals assisted with the daily routines of the household, were exceptionally dedicated to the care of the horses and other pets, and welcomed guests who were treasured as their own.

The halls of Hartwood are now empty of the family's footsteps that once graced them, but they continue to ring with the melodic sound of laughter, an appreciation for architectural enchantment, and an entirely new set of caretakers who call the estate home. With the utmost respect and reverence, I wish to acknowledge the ceaseless dedication of the current caretakers, including Patti Benaglio and the many other volunteers who carry on the legacy begun by the Lawrence family. I also extend my gratitude to the descendants of the Lawrence and Flinn families for the privilege of sharing their stories. Unless otherwise noted, all images contained herein appear courtesy of Hartwood Mansion.

I am thankful to my parents and friends who are truly my family for their unending support in ways both great and small.

Lastly, and with immeasurable appreciation and love, I wish to mostly humbly thank my beloved daughter Bekah. You are my inspiration, my dedication, and my light that shines on brighter days ahead. May the halls of your heart always have a place to call home, and may you always know how grateful I am that you have been mine.

INTRODUCTION

AUTHOR'S NOTE: Throughout this publication, the residence itself is referred to as both "Hartwood" and "Hartwood Acres." These denote two very different lineages in the history of the house. During the time that the Lawrence family was in residence, they referred to their personal estate simply as "Hartwood." When the property and residence were purchased by Allegheny County and opened to the public in 1976, the newly accessible house and grounds were thereafter referred to as "Hartwood Acres." In order to maintain historical accuracy when referring to specific time periods, "Hartwood" will refer to the home as a family residence while "Hartwood Acres" will refer to the residence and grounds as a portion of the Allegheny County parks system.

Hartwood was a house that started as a dream. Inspired by an English country estate that Mary Flinn Lawrence and her husband, John, once visited, the idea of what could be began to form in Mary's mind. As a scioness of well-known Pittsburgh construction firm Booth and Flinn (spearheaded by her father, [later senator] William Flinn), Mary was familiar with many of the ins and outs of building something from the ground up. Her father's company built much of the infrastructure in the city of Pittsburgh during the burgeoning decades of the 20th century. Mary took what she learned in her early life and applied it to actively participate in the decision-making process for building the home where she eventually built her family as well.

Upon the death of Senator Flinn in 1924, Mary Flinn Lawrence inherited a great deal of wealth from her father's business ventures, which provided the means for her to pursue her own dreams. Hartwood was the recognition and realization of those notions. Her father's legacy afforded Mary the ability to purchase approximately 479 acres in the hillsides above Indiana and Hampton Townships just outside of Pittsburgh, Pennsylvania. Today, that footprint has been expanded to include approximately 629 acres for the general public to explore.

In 1974, Mary Flinn Lawrence died. Upon her death, the Allegheny County park system took over ownership of the estate with a few stipulations. Mary decreed that the land would never be subdivided and that members of the original household be allowed to remain on the grounds. Beyond that, the majority of the home retains the family's original possessions, right down to the finest silverware from Mary's childhood home and treasured antiques that the Lawrences collected throughout the years.

One of the finest representations of this is the paneling in the Great Hall itself. Brought specifically to Hartwood from a 1600s English estate (Lee Hall in Oxfordshire, England), the paneling compliments many of the fine details of the home's grandest room. On display at Hartwood Acres are a fine Flemish tapestry dating to the 17th century, a hand-carved mantle that dates to the 1600s, and a stone fireplace with Tudor roses that originated during the Middle Ages. Each of these is just a sampling of what can be seen during a tour of the inside of the home.

The grounds of the estate now continue to teem with those who enjoy the myriad of trails, tranquil serenity, and numerous outdoor activities the landscape still provides. An ardent conservationist,

Mary Flinn Lawrence ensured the perpetual integrity of these grounds by initiating the planting of 96,000 pine saplings throughout the acreage surrounding the home. Just down from the main residence, the stables remain as a testament to the rich equestrian history, which is imprinted upon the grounds. Numerous competitions took place in the decades when the Lawrence family first resided there. The Lawrences competed alongside other prominent families of the area and often hosted an annual fox hunt which was one of the premier social events in the area. These traditions are still woven into the fabric of Hartwood Acres today, representing both a bygone era and the Lawrence family itself.

As the crown jewel of the Allegheny County park system, Hartwood Acres is today staffed by a dedicated and caring group of individuals who ensure the preservation of the stories of the home and the priceless items contained within. Thousands visit each year to see the intricate stained-glass windows, the hand-painted walls, the painting that John Lawrence left unfinished at the time of his passing, and the books that the Lawrences' sons once shared next to a roaring fireplace.

Today, the park encompasses many aspects and facets that once belonged to the Lawrence family alone. With grace and foresight, Mary Flinn Lawrence ensured that generations to come could enjoy both the finest grandeur and a quiet escape from daily life.

As we turn back the pages of its history, we have been granted unrestricted archival access through the generosity of Hartwood Acres manager Patti Benaglio and her dedicated staff and volunteers. The images contained in this work capture intimate moments, such as mothers tenderly cradling their newborn infants, the windswept moments of a family vacation near the seashore, and the heartbreaking details of a wartime chaplain's letter that arrived too late to say goodbye.

While parents John and Mary, along with their sons Johnny and Billy, were the only family to call the house home, the lives of their parents, siblings, and others who were essential to the history of Hartwood are also presented here. Their stories are interwoven, and each has its place in the pages of history told within these walls.

As you travel through these pages, you share the journeys they each took throughout their lifetimes. With John's untimely passing at the age of 54, Mary suddenly became a single mother to their two young sons Johnny and Billy, then ages eleven and eight, respectively. With an air of dignified grace and dedication to bettering the lives of children everywhere, Mary embodied a philanthropic legacy that remains to this day.

We continue this legacy in sharing their stories as we visually walk past the wooded trails and stables, through the flowers of the garden, and throughout the sunlit halls of the home once known as Hartwood.

One

BUILDING BRIDGES

Before the physical foundations of the family home known as Hartwood were poured, the financial foundations were put in place. As the daughter of Pittsburgh's William Flinn and his wife, Nancy Galbraith Flinn, Mary Flinn Lawrence was born a member of the social elite. Her father was a senator and a well-known businessman. Flinn's construction firm Booth and Flinn was responsible for much of the infrastructure throughout the city of Pittsburgh and beyond. Booth and Flinn was associated with notable structures such as Pittsburgh's McKees Rocks Bridge, Armstrong Tunnels, Wabash Tunnels, Liberty Tubes, and the George Westinghouse Memorial Bridge. Upon her father's death, Mary inherited the financial means that made the construction of her dream home possible. Hartwood arose from foundations such as these, and it is impossible to tell the story of one without first paying tribute to the building blocks that came before.

BRIDGING THE GAP. The construction giant of the Booth and Flinn Company, under the leadership of William Flinn, was an industrial force in the city of Pittsburgh in the early half of the 20th century. Major projects such as the North Side Point Bridge (also known as the Manchester Bridge) were created through the efforts of the company, and the many blue-collar workers who devoted their lives to the work. This structure spanned the Monongahela River near "the Point" in downtown Pittsburgh from 1915 to 1969. It was then decommissioned and torn down a year later. Pictured here in the year that it closed, the North Side Point Bridge (Manchester Bridge) was a shining example of the influence that the Booth and Flinn Company had on the infrastructure of Pittsburgh. Another major influence in the city can be seen just to the right of the bridge: Pittsburgh's own nascent Three Rivers Stadium, which opened the same year the bridge was torn down. (Both, Library of Congress.)

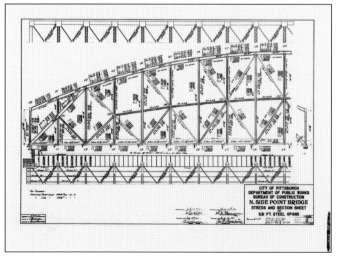

BUILDING BLOCKS. The image above from the Library of Congress shows the west end arch of the McKees Rocks Bridge in Pittsburgh. The bridge itself was built in 1931, with the famous Pittsburgh construction firm Booth and Flinn responsible for the approach ramps onto the bridge. The elder statesman of the company, William Flinn (Mary's father), passed away in 1924, several years before the bridge was completed. The numerous successful projects of the Booth and Flinn Company such as the McKees Rocks and Liberty Bridge (below) eventually laid the framework for much of the family's wealth, which ultimately provided the means for Mary to build her home at Hartwood. (Both, Library of Congress.)

CROSSROADS. As shown in the image above, documented in 1997 by photographer Joseph Elliott, the north approach of the Liberty Bridge (looking east) remains an essential and recognizable intersection in Pittsburgh's downtown area. As with many critical pieces of Pittsburgh's infrastructure, this span was built by Booth and Flinn (the firm belonging to Mary's father). The firm also built the George Westinghouse Bridge, shown to the left. Sharing a close relationship with her father, Mary was exposed to many aspects of building and construction that served her well as she eventually applied that knowledge to building the Hartwood estate. (Both, Library of Congress.)

Two

THE HEART
OF HARTWOOD

It was filled with light, predicated on lifelong dreams, and built to be cherished for generations. Although this could easily apply to the house known as Hartwood, it is ever more true for the very heart of what made the house a home—the family who resided within. Mary and her husband, John, shared the home together for nearly a decade before adopting Johnny, the first of their two sons. Billy, their second adopted son, joined the family soon afterward. For the next seven years, the family enjoyed holiday events, equestrian competitions, and quiet moments spent together in the family library. In 1945, however, John died at the age of 54, leaving Mary as a single mother to two young sons. In the years that followed, they continued to fill the home with loving memories which still resonate throughout the pages of Hartwood's history today.

POSED AND POISED. These portraits of a young Mary Flinn date to approximately the turn of the 20th century. Families of the day frequently captured images such as this. Several fine examples of Flinn family portraits remain in the archives of Hartwood Acres. While the specific photographer for these images is unknown, they were taken during the time Mary lived with her family in their Braemar estate near present-day Highland Park.

A WORK OF ART. The March 27, 1909, *Pittsburgh Post Gazette* lauded the charitable efforts of a young Mary Flinn. As president of her local Young Women's Christian Association, Flinn arranged to host a tableaux vivant—a sort of "living pictures" show to benefit the organization. Society girls partook in a pantomime mimicking famous paintings, which was accompanied by a live symphony performing classical music as the crowds passed by. Six displays were shown, including the work of John Singer Sargent, Sir Joshua Reynolds, and Sir Lawrence Alma Tadema. The high society event was one of many charitable efforts Flinn supported, even at a young age. She is shown here just left of center alongside a group of her close friends of the time.

Social Circles. Young Mary Flinn, shown first row on the far right, was raised as a member of Pittsburgh's upper class. Mary's brother Ralph Flinn is also pictured in this image, standing directly behind Mary at far right in the top row. Mary participated in many social events, such as the wedding of Baroness Margaret Louise Magee Riedl de Ridenau, the bride pictured here at center. The social circles of Pittsburgh at the time included many notable names, such as Mellon, Frick, Magee, and Heinz—the last of which were often guests of the Flinn and Lawrence families throughout the years.

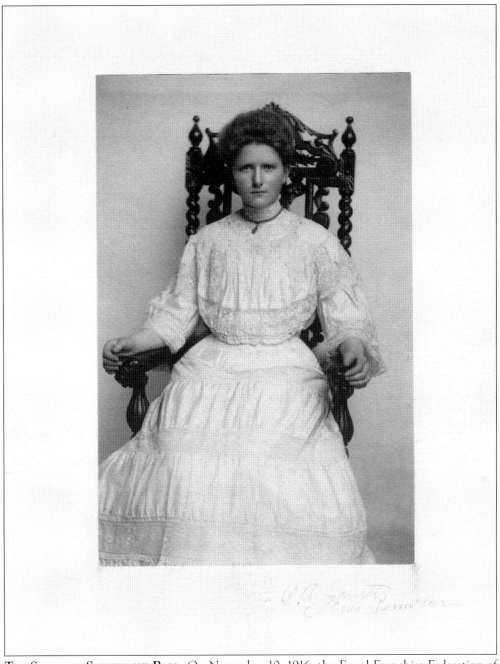

The Suffrage Shirtwaist Ball. On November 10, 1916, the Equal Franchise Federation of Pittsburgh (of which Mary Flinn Lawrence was a founding member) held its Suffrage Shirtwaist Ball at the Motor Square Garden in the East Liberty neighborhood of Pittsburgh. It was gloriously well attended, with over 3,000 people showing up to support the cause. The attendees consisted not only of women supporting the cause but also students, politicians, working-class men and women, and various representatives of the social strata. The event capped numerous efforts by the organization in support of giving women the right to vote. The evening's singular and incredibly successful turnout raised $2,500 at the time—equivalent to $65,000 today.

WINTER BY THE SEA. Possibly owing to the family's status, it is fortunate that so many photographs of them were taken, and that so many remain to this day. In an exemplification of the family's stature, photographs representing a number of locales are interspersed throughout the family ephemera. Imprinted with the name of the photography studio— the Carlin Studios, of 1107 Boardwalk, Atlantic City, New Jersey—this image can be identified and dated to around 1900, when this studio along with many others welcomed tourists to the small seaside town. Interestingly, this does not appear to have been the typical summer vacation, as Mary Flinn is shown dressed in a heavy coat with fur trim and a winter muff to protect her from the cold breeze carried in off the nearby ocean.

HATS OFF. In an image that drips with opulence, a very young Mary Flinn is shown at approximately age 12. The portrait, surrounded by an ornate gilded frame, was one of many formal portraits the Flinn family had taken of their children. Dressed in the finest attire, Mary's pensive eyes gaze out under a bonnet featuring beautifully detailed silk adornments.

MAKING A HABIT OF IT. Displaying poise and character from a very young age, Mary Flinn is shown here in a traditional riding habit. It is one of the iconic images of Flinn's younger years. She devoted the rest of her life to showmanship, equestrian achievements, and sharing her love of both the sport and horses with her own sons Johnny and Billy (shown below) when she eventually raised a family of her own.

THE BRIARCLIFF SIX. These images appeared in a scrapbook that belonged to Harry Lawrence (brother of Mary's husband, John Lawrence). In the image above, a group of women who are noted in the margins of the photo album as the "Briarcliff Six" enjoys time visiting in upstate New York. Mary attended school in Briarcliff Manor, New York, and is pictured here with girls who were likely her schoolmates. In the image below, Mary (background, right) enjoys a candid moment between friends in the countryside.

MARY AT BEECHWOOD. The site where this photograph was taken, Beechwood, originally belonged to Mary Flinn's father, William Flinn. In 1977, a total of 90 acres of farmland were donated to the Western Pennsylvania Conservancy by Rachel Lariman Mellon Walton, Joshua C. Whetzel Jr., and Farley Walton Whetzel. At that time, the Audubon Society of Western Pennsylvania began to manage the property, which serves as a nature center. The intervening years have seen some changes and additions to the site, but today it functions much as it did at the beginning of the 20th century—as a place of beauty and nature and as a protected environmental oasis for the many animals and people who still enjoy the grounds to this day.

QUEENS OF COOL. While sparse in the background, the details in this image encapsulate the effortless cool of a bygone era. Mary Flinn Lawrence is pictured with an unidentified female friend. The women both sport lovely hats, with Mary's trimmed in a floral fabric matching the rest of her attire. The Lawrence family was known to have a varying collection of notable vehicles, perhaps including the one shown here.

CONSTANT COMPANION. This simple but striking image shows Mary Flinn with one of the many beloved dogs she shared her home with during her lifetime. Based on contextual evidence from other photographs in the archives, it is believed that this image was taken shortly before the time of Flinn's wedding, which occurred in 1914. What appears to be the same dog (a borzoi) based on his coloration and height also appears in Flinn's engagement photograph, which was taken at her childhood home of Braemar. Throughout her lifetime, Mary Flinn was surrounded by both family and pets, many of whom were lovingly shared in the same photographs together.

ENDEARING AND ENGAGING. The remarkable nature of this image is not immediately understood from its luminous composition alone. Several features make this one of the most memorable images in the Hartwood Acres archives. This is the engagement portrait of Mary Flinn, taken prior to her marriage to John Lawrence in 1914. The image was captured in Flinn's childhood home, Braemar, where the couple celebrated their wedding reception and lived for a time while their eventual home, Hartwood, was under construction. The dog pictured at her side is a borzoi, which was noted for being associated with Russian aristocracy prior to the downfall of imperial rule under the Romanovs. On an even more personal note, throughout the years, this photograph sat on John Lawrence's nightstand next to his bed and remains displayed at Hartwood in that same location to this day.

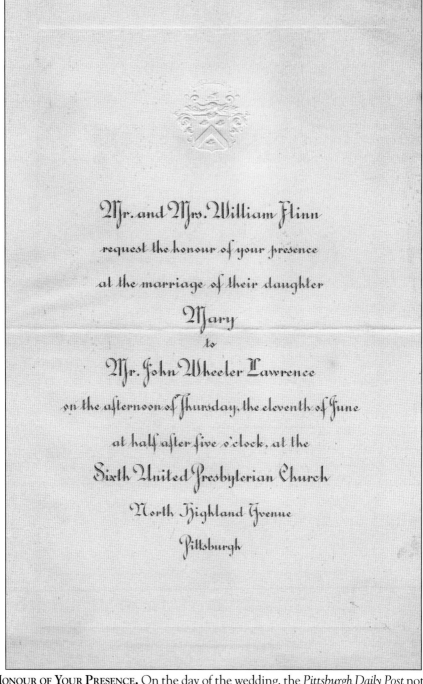

Mr. and Mrs. William Flinn

request the honour of your presence

at the marriage of their daughter

Mary

to

Mr. John Wheeler Lawrence

on the afternoon of Thursday, the eleventh of June

at half after five o'clock, at the

Sixth United Presbyterian Church

North Highland Avenue

Pittsburgh

THE HONOUR OF YOUR PRESENCE. On the day of the wedding, the *Pittsburgh Daily Post* noted that "Miss Edith G. Flinn will act as her sister's maid of honor." The following day, the same paper declared the event a success, and described the "pulpit decorated as an exquisite garden." Many other members of the family comprised the wedding party, and the couple later stopped to visit none other than family friend Teddy Roosevelt at Sagamore Hill in Cove Neck, New York, near Oyster Bay during the course of their honeymoon.

To Have and to Hold. With her sister Edith standing by as her maid of honor, Mary Flinn became Mary Lawrence when she married John Lawrence on June 11, 1914. Harry J. Lawrence Jr. (brother of the groom) served as his best man. The wedding took place in Pittsburgh's Sixth United Presbyterian Church. The bridal gown had been beautifully detailed and was trimmed in pearls, with layers of tulle throughout. It was further decorated with orange blossoms, and two small diamond pins to hold her veil in place. Within her hands, Mary carried a bouquet of exquisite yellow roses carefully tended to and grown on the Flinn family farm, Beechwood. Following the wedding, a reception for 350 people was held at Braemar—the family's home. Name cards for the guests glittered with gold lettering. A pavilion had been built especially for the event, with an orchestra from New York providing the entertainment. In the center of the bridal table stood a fountain filled with Killarney roses and water lilies. This particular detail can still be seen today. The fountain that once graced their bridal table remains within the Hartwood Mansion, proudly displayed to guests today, much as it was at their wedding on June 11, 1914.

Mrs. John Wheeler Lawrence

Hartwood
Pittsburgh 38

WHEN MARY COMES CALLING. This simple calling card, both intricate and refined in its detailing, cannot fully convey the nature of the era in which it was used. Popular for centuries, calling cards such as these were first used in France in the 1700s. They were especially popular among the upper echelon as a means of recognizing various events of significance in a family's life. These included congratulations, gratitude, and mourning, as well as indicating a desire to visit a particular individual or a family as a whole. The inclusion of both "Mrs. John Wheeler Lawrence" and "Hartwood" on this card allows us to date Mary Flinn Lawrence's use of it to the years following the construction of the home in 1929.

TRAVELS THROUGH TIME. While it is unknown which adventure this ship was taking her to, it is certain that Mary Flinn Lawrence and her family enjoyed many travels throughout the years. The archives of Hartwood Acres contain several family photo albums documenting trips throughout upstate New York and the Jersey Shore, along with more remote locations that appear to be mountainous or out west. In the image at right, Mary appears to be wearing a wedding ring, likely dating these images to sometime between 1914 (when she was married) and the early 1920s.

THROUGH THE ARTIST'S EYES. This delicate pencil portrait of Mary Flinn Lawrence must surely have been well-liked by its subject. The sketch was preserved in her papers, and she selected it for her passport, dated February 5, 1926, when she was 38 years old. The original sketch is hand-signed by the artist, William Van Dresser. The world knew his name. Van Dresser's paintings and sketches included commissions from two US presidents (Calvin Coolidge and Franklin D. Roosevelt). A family genealogical volume from 1915 noted Van Dresser as an "artist of ability who illustrates for all the leading magazines and is also an illustrator of books. He inherited his artistic ability from his mother. He has studied in Chicago, Illinois, New York City and Paris, and has taught in the Art Students' League of New York City." Jack London's 1916 novel *The Little Lady of the Big House* featured Van Dresser's art on the cover.

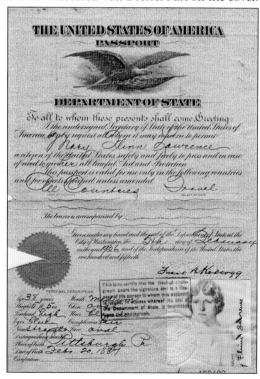

PRETTY AS A PICTURE. Likely along with the same borzoi dog that appeared in her engagement photos, Mary Flinn Lawrence is pictured here in this pastoral setting holding an early version of the Kodak folding cameras which were popular at the time. Nearly 100 years after the first photograph was taken in 1826, cameras in the early 1900s had become widely available, and amateur photography was all the rage. Both portable and easy to use, these cameras became the means by which memories of everyday life were captured by families. Fortunately, many of the images the Flinn and Lawrence families preserved during this time remain in the archives of Hartwood Acres and have been included in this very publication.

FIT FOR A QUEEN. In 1926, at the request of Gifford Pinchot (28th governor of Pennsylvania from 1931–1935), Mary Flinn Lawrence accompanied a gathering of women to meet in New York. The trip heralded the arrival of a very important guest—Queen Marie of Romania—aboard the SS *Leviathan*. Mary's role was to join the queen and two of her children (Prince Nicholas and Princess Ileana) as they journeyed to Washington, DC, to meet then Pres. Calvin Coolidge. The queen later continued her diplomatic visit to towns across the United States. Mary is shown here, her statuesque form accented by her lengthy diamond necklace, in her official capacity with the royal retinue during the queen's visit.

Trinity Court Photo

Mrs. John W. Lawrence of "Hartwood Farm"

SIBLING RIVALRY. Cutting a striking portrait in a cloche hat, Mary Flinn Lawrence is seen here in an excerpt from the *Pittsburgh Sun-Telegraph* of April 17, 1928. The article spoke to Mary's political prowess as she supported James M. Magee for Congress. Her brother George H. Flinn, however, supported opposing candidate Congressman Harry A. Estep. Mary threatened against political corruption, noting "Election officers who take orders and try to steal the election . . . are looking a jail term in the face." Estep went on to defeat Magee in the election.

ALONG FOR THE RIDE. In a locale that is decidedly not her hometown of Pittsburgh (based on the palm trees in the background), Mary Flinn is pictured with her sister Edith taking a journey in a rattan rickshaw. The Flinn and Lawrence families were known to enjoy holiday vacations at the shore, and methods of transportation such as this were very popular in tourist towns at the time. Given the young appearance of the sisters, it is likely that this image dates to the very early part of the 20th century, which coincides with many of the other vacation photographs held in the family's private archival collection.

DRIVING FORCE. Mary Flinn was strong, outspoken, courageous, and assertive. She was so many things that people said a woman of the time should not be. She faced notions telling women they could not or should not, but she did things her way. She stood on her own against the constraints of a time when women were barely able to drive or vote and did both with grace. Shown here with one of Pittsburgh's well-known Harper sisters (possibly Electra), Mary was clearly adept at not only social skills but also mechanical efforts. It is believed that the two are in the process of changing a tire, likely before setting off on a new adventure.

DAPPER DAYS. A young John Lawrence strikes a dashing figure in this archival image from Hartwood around 1910. Success followed him throughout his life as he dedicated himself to many noble efforts. The young man shown here eventually served his country in both World War I and World War II. During World War I, he served as an ensign in the Navy. He was later commissioned in the Air Corps in World War II and served at both Fort George Wright in Spokane, Washington, and at the Salt Lake City Army Air Corps classification base. John and his wife, Mary, were ardent supporters of the military and often hosted benefits for the war effort. John served as the first president of the United War Fund and was the president of the board at the Federation of Social Agencies. He was also a chairman of the US Committee for the Care of European Children—a cause notably close to his heart, as both of his own children were adopted from Europe.

JOHN LAWRENCE WITH BI-PLANE
BENDIST FLYING BOAT
c. 1912-1913

THE BENOIST FLYING BOAT. For a very short time between 1913 and 1914, the Benoist biplane (pictured here with John Lawrence in 1912–1913) served as one of the very first commercial methods of air transport in the United States. Only two were ever built, and the service was discontinued within one year of its initial founding, as the funding for the project became unavailable. While it is unclear if Lawrence actually utilized this as a means of transport, there were also opportunities to see the planes as part of a traveling tourist attraction that once visited Conneaut Lake in Northwestern Pennsylvania.

ON THE ROAD TO RECOVERY. The road shown here in front of the stables is one that the Lawrence family traversed often. John Lawrence served as master of foxhounds at the Fox Chapel Hunt. In 1935, although bedridden with a broken ankle, he continued his efforts toward the ever-important affair by making the arrangements for an upcoming event from his hospital bed at Pittsburgh's West Penn Hospital. "To think how many times I have fallen through fences, and had horses kick me, and jumpers roll over on me without getting seriously hurt, and then this silly accident," Lawrence was quoted as saying in the June 9, 1935, *Pittsburgh Sun-Telegraph*. His diligent dedication was evident, however, when the Junior Horse Show took place the following week near the family's Hartwood estate stables, shown here.

A MOTHER'S LOVE. Mary Flinn Lawrence and her husband, John Lawrence, became parents when they were both in their late 40s. After reaching out to numerous adoption agencies, they were informed of the birth of John Frederick Scott (later named John Wheeler Lawrence Jr.). Born in 1934, he traveled to America in 1938 and was adopted by the Lawrences that spring—approximately around the time these images were captured.

JOHNNY LAWRENCE. Born in Essex, England, on June 11, 1934, John Wheeler "Johnny" Lawrence Jr. was the first of two boys that John and Mary Flinn Lawrence adopted. Young Johnny spent his childhood at Hartwood and often rode horses both as a hobby and competitively. As an adult, he attended Delaware Valley College and served his country in the US Army. In 1966, Johnny moved from Pittsburgh to the Grove City area, where he tended the land for years as a farmer until his passing on December 21, 2011, at the age of 77.

A PEACEFUL RESPITE. Embraced by both their mother, Mary, and the loving home they shared, John W. Lawrence Jr. and William F. Lawrence enjoyed quiet moments such as this at the family's Hartwood estate. In the present day, this location hosts numerous weddings, events, and social gatherings. At this moment, however, the family was surrounded by the lush greenery, gardens, and the serenity of a simple moment in time.

THE BONDS OF BROTHERHOOD. Both of the Lawrence brothers, Johnny and Billy, came to the family by means of adoption. While much is known about both the circumstance and background of Johnny's birth family, much less is known about Billy's. The elder brother sought out his birth mother in adulthood. They maintained a relationship, and she came to the United States several times to visit from her native England. Billy's background had been likewise affected by the horrors of the Nazis during World War II. Born in France in 1937, Billy was adopted into the family three years later in 1940. He never sought out his birth family. In *Reflections of Hartwood*, Jeffrey S. Lawrence notes that "John would recall that shortly after William arrived in the United States William would dive under the grand piano in the great room when he heard planes fly over the mansion." Later in life, John became a farmer in Grove City, Pennsylvania. William was a professor at West Virginia University until retiring to the Florida Keys.

SIDE BY SIDE. Mary Flinn Lawrence was very involved in the care and upbringing of her two young sons, Johnny and Billy. From a very young age, she acquainted them with the finer points of equestrian events and showmanship. This image, taken during an event in 1940, shows Mary riding sidesaddle on one of her beloved horses. A young John Heinz looks after Mary as he sits astride his very own horse.

A Boy's Best Friend. In a photograph that is both timeless and touching, a young Billy Lawrence is shown with one of the family's faithful companions. Warm family photographs such as these are sprinkled throughout the family's archives, and speak to the intimate nature of their dynamic. Although the home was the scene of numerous social, political, and community events, quiet moments such as these resonate throughout the generations to capture the joy and bond shared between a child and his faithful companion.

OUTDOOR PETS. The grounds of Hartwood teemed with wildlife. Situated on hundreds of acres, the encompassing woodlands created a safe haven for the many deer, fox, birds, rabbits, and raccoons that enjoyed the abundance of the streams and blossoms that dotted the sylvan landscape. Occasionally, the boys enjoyed interactions such as this touching family image of Johnny Lawrence bottle-feeding a pet raccoon near the family's homestead.

THE BONDS OF FRIENDSHIP. The influential friendships cultivated by Mary's father, Sen. William Flinn, continued long after his death in 1924. At the close of the following decade, Mary and her husband, John Lawrence, began the process of adopting their two children, Johnny and Billy Lawrence. In this image, Johnny is shown enjoying an informal riding lesson along with a family friend. That friend was from a family that was a household name in Pittsburgh, and the child later became a recognized name in his own right. Shown here in the striped shirt is Henry John Heinz III, who became a US senator until his untimely death in 1991 as the result of a plane crash. The two boys were lifelong friends and served as the best men at each other's weddings.

ONE WOMAN'S VOICE. The women's suffrage movement was a cause that was very near to Mary Flinn Lawrence's heart. She campaigned tirelessly on behalf of women everywhere who were struggling to have their voices heard. An ardent political activist, and having been raised in a political household, Mary had a unique understanding of what it took to balance both ambition and societal nuances. As a founding member of the Equal Franchise Federation of Pittsburgh, Mary was making strides toward women's rights nearly a full decade before the ratification of the 19th Amendment in August 1920.

Born in Pittsburgh, Pennsylvania, daughter of the late Honorable and Mrs. William Flinn. Attended school at Farmington, Connecticut, and Mrs. Dow's at Briarcliff Manor, New York. Married June 11, 1914. Active in Philanthropy and Civic affairs since very young and Politics as a matter of training under her Father, who was for many years the Republican Leader of Pittsburgh and Pennsylvania, and later one of the founders and prominent leaders of the Progressive Party, and close personal fiend of Theodore Roosevelt. Mrs. Lawrence took a very active part in the Woman Suffrage cause for several years in Pennsylvania, being an official of the Association. She has done much public speaking, both political and for various causes, and during the war was an Intructress in the Red Cross and officer in the Medical Corps. Her father organized the first Commission for the relief in Belgium, and was decorated by King Albert when he visited Pittsburgh. Mrs. Lawrence was appointed by Governor Sproul to the first Womans Republican State Committee, and helped organize the Pennsylvania Council of Republican Women, being Vice-President since its origin five years ago. Elected member of the Republican State Committee. She is prominent as an Independent Republican and took a prominent part in the election of Gifford Pinchot, as Governor of Pennsylvania. She has worked very actively for the cause of clean elections and served as Vice-Chairman of the Committee of 76 of Pennsylvania, which played an active part in Election Reform. She has been a member appointed by three Governors of the Pennsylvania State Forest Commissionsince 1920. Also appointed by the Governor as member of the Children's Commission and served as Vice-Chairman. This Commission studies all Laws relating to children in Pennsylvania, and recommended changes and had passed several valuable laws on Adoption, Indenture, etc. She was appointed one ofthe women to represent Pennsylvania in welcoming Queen Marie of Roumania in the United States. Is a member of the Advisory Council of the Pennsylvania Department of Labor and Industry, served as Vice-Chairman of Pennsylvania Christmas Red Cross Seal Committee; is Vice-Chairman of Industrial Home for Crippled Children, Harmarville Convalescent Home, AssociatedCharities of Pittsburgh, Pittsburgh Skin and Cancer Foundation, Pennsylvania Elections Association. She is a member of the following clubs: Colony, New York; Women's National Republican Club, Pittsburgh Golf Club, Allegheny County Club, Fox Chapel Club, Rolling Rock Club, and a member and active worker in Trinity Episcopal Church. Recreations - ardent horsewoman, riding to hounds, tennis, swimming and skating.

A LIFE WELL LIVED. By context, this article summarizing Mary Flinn Lawrence's life dates to 1928. It mentions that she helped organize the Pennsylvania Council of Republican Women (five years ago), an organization that was founded in 1923. So many of Mary's accomplishments are noted here, including her appointment to represent Pennsylvania during a visit from Queen Marie of Romania. Much of Mary's political work is encapsulated in this documentation, which possibly was written by Mary herself as an introduction to one of the many social or political organizations she was affiliated with.

MARY'S CHARITIES. In her younger years, Mary Flinn was first introduced to her father's work with the (then-called) Industrial Home for Crippled Children. The influence of that volunteer work was far-reaching, lasting throughout her lifetime. It was the beginning of many philanthropic endeavors to which she devoted herself. Specifically, Mary served as the vice president of the Industrial Home for Crippled Children, a role that earned her a nomination on the "Distinguished Citizen Ballot" in the April 13, 1930, *Pittsburgh Press* newspaper. Later that month, she became one of only two women who were ultimately selected to receive the honor. Mary's work with the group continued for decades, and she is pictured here midcentury with one of the children to whom she so generously devoted her time and efforts.

IN SUPPORT OF THE CAUSE. Founded in 1881 by Clara Barton, the Red Cross was innately involved with supporting US troops during World War II. It was a cause that Mary Flinn Lawrence cared greatly for, and she is shown here in a Red Cross Uniform in the early 1940s. Her participation with the organization was just one of many ways she dedicated herself to activism throughout her lifetime.

THE BLUSHING BRIDE. Although decades removed from her 1914 wedding to John Lawrence, Mary Flinn Lawrence is shown here outside of Hartwood, wearing the wedding gown that she undoubtedly treasured throughout the years. Other images in the archives show her at this same event but pictured with her husband, John, dating this photograph prior to 1945, when he passed from complications resulting from a broken femur. The couple had shared 31 years of marriage together.

INFLUENTIAL FRIENDS. Mary Flinn Lawrence's social and political circles were often intertwined, and both were known to include some very influential people. Mary dedicated herself to numerous causes on behalf of the Republican Party during the course of her lifetime and even served as the secretary of the commonwealth under Gifford Pinchot of the Progressive Party. Her intelligence and resourcefulness allowed her to hold her own in a world that once would not have even allowed her to vote.

MORE THAN MEETS THE EYE. This formalized portrait of Mary Flinn Lawrence represents one of several publicity stills she had taken throughout her lifetime. As a patron of many philanthropic endeavors, Mary was affiliated with numerous charitable groups throughout Pittsburgh and often appeared in both the newspaper and in literature for those various organizations. Of particular note is the inscribed "Parry" signature on the bottom-right of this image. Parry Studio operated in Pittsburgh, Pennsylvania, from 1922 to 1950. The photographer set up shop in the city's notable William Penn Hotel and was well known for their numerous society portraits of the day. The photographer was no stranger to intermingling with the elite, having spent a number of years gracing the stages of New York before marrying and moving to Pittsburgh in 1915. What was unusual about this photographer is likely what drew Mary Flinn's support, as she focused much of her energy on various women's issues. The person behind the camera—Florence Fisher Parry—was one of a very small handful of successful female photographers operating in Pittsburgh during that time.

· AUG · 57

FAMILY FRIENDS. The home at Hartwood was always full of life and love, both for its two-legged companions and the four-legged variety. Taken in August 1957 when Mary Flinn Lawrence was 70 years old, this image reflects a quiet moment on one of the estate's outdoor patios. In a home where every detail was appointed with the utmost care, even the outdoor patio furniture was hand-crafted by artisans using the most ornate wrought iron and intricate tile work. Lush greenery and florals complemented the outdoor space, likely cultivated from the nearby gardens which graced the grounds.

AN OUTSTANDING WOMAN. In 1959, Mary Flinn Lawrence was honored with the distinction of being named as one of the Outstanding Women of the Year in the *Pittsburgh Post-Gazette*. The attribution was received as a result of Mary's decades of work supporting neglected children and children with disabilities. Appointed by Gifford Pinchot as a vice-chairperson of an organization that supported these efforts, Mary proved to be an outspoken advocate for both the legal representation and well-being of children. The award also recognized her numerous efforts to protect the natural landscape of Pennsylvania's parks, rest stops, and forests. In addition to protecting her home state, Mary dedicated her efforts to protect her country during World War II. She served with the American Women's Voluntary Service and sold millions of dollars worth of war bonds, which benefited the country. A December 31, 1959, *Pittsburgh Post-Gazette* article notes that Mary "received recognition from the British War Relief Society, the National Institute of Social Sciences, and Pennsylvania Citizen's Association, which she helped to incorporate." She was a woman who tirelessly strove to better the lives of others around her and left lasting impressions as she did so.

Registered under the Adoption of Children
(Regulation) Act. 1939.

THE NATIONAL ADOPTION SOCIETY.

(Registered under the Friendly Societies' Act. 1896 to 1979)

President : Lady Gweneth Cavendish.
Vice-President : The Countess of Bessborough.
Chairman : Mrs. Gerald Glover.
Appeals Organiser : Colonel Ivo Reid, O.B.E.

47a, Manchester Street, Nr. Baker St.,
LONDON, W.1.

March 1960

Dear ꞏꞏꞏꞏꞏꞏꞏꞏ,

Since the day when you adopted your baby with our assistance we have
year by year been continuing our efforts as best we can. Certainly the
need for our work has in no way diminished; more unlucky children are born
into the world each year, who must be found responsible parents like your-
selves to look after them rather than be left without the advantages of the
love and security of a family and home. We know only too well from our
own records the vast numbers of couples who so want a child to complete
their family but cannot have one of their own.

However, we are hampered at present from filling this need as well
as we should like for the lack of two different services, which we really
feel are essential, both of which as you may imagine need considerable
financial support.   First, we desperately need to reopen our own Hostel
staffed with medically trained personnel, where an expectant mother can
come before and after the birth of her child rather than having to live
in unsuitable lodgings or an unhappy home atmosphere.   Secondly, as an
alternative we need to organise an efficient foster mother service so that
babies can be looked after properly during the necessary six weeks before
adoption.   Although official approval is forthcoming for our efforts -
local authorities would be prepared to pay for individual cases coming to
the hostel - we can get no initial financial assistance towards reopening
the hostel, nor can we hope for any grant or allowance towards maintaining
or subsidising a foster mother service.

You can therefore appreciate how much we need funds to start both
branches of our service and we feel we shall not be disappointed if we
appeal to you with your special knowledge of our problems for even the
most modest contributions, say five or ten shillings, towards the fund we
are opening.   We should of course be delighted if you felt sufficiently
interested to keep in touch with us by becoming a subscriber to our Society,
and for this purpose we will send on request a Bankers Order for our annual
subscription of one guinea in return for which we shall keep you fully informed of all our activities, and invite you to come to any social events
we shall be organising in the future.

Yours sincerely,

Susan g'love

PHILANTHROPIC ENDEAVORS. Following the death of her husband, John, and in the intervening years since their own children had been adopted, Mary continued to support numerous philanthropic efforts dedicated to bettering the lives of children. In March 1960, this donation solicitation letter was received from the National Adoption Society. The president of the organization is noted on the letterhead as Lady Gweneth Cavendish, a woman who had been instrumental in John and Mary's adoption of their own children.

Three

BRANCHES OF THE TREE

The Flinn and Lawrence families were joined with the union of John Wheeler Lawrence and Mary Stephen Flinn on June 11, 1914. The two shared a tender closeness with their family including their parents, siblings, and some very influential family friends such as Teddy Roosevelt and Gifford Pinchot. In addition to blood relatives, many of the caretakers at Hartwood became as close to the Lawrences as their own family members. Intermingled alongside the storied lives of John, Mary, and their children are those they held quite close at heart. Shared within this chapter are stories of Mary's parents, William and Nancy Flinn, and her siblings including Edith, George, Ralph, A. Rex, and Arthur. John's family is also detailed through treasured family photographs. Letters represent heartbreakingly intimate details of wartime tragedy and immeasurable courage. Also interspersed among the branches are stories of caretakers like Stanley Prostrednik, who lovingly tended the family's exquisite gardens. Each of these lives grew as leaves often do, with their traces remaining long after the seasons have passed.

FOR NEARLY 50 YEARS.
William Flinn and Nancy
Galbraith were married
in 1874 and remained so
until Senator Flinn's death
on February 19, 1924. At
the time, they had been
married for nearly 50 years.
His family immigrated
from England in the early
1850s. She was born in
Butler, Pennsylvania, on
July 20, 1851. Together,
the Flinns built a legacy of
both business and family,
in which the two were
often intertwined. Their
children (seven born, six
surviving to adulthood)
created their own
prominent legacies and
left their imprint through
their careers, philanthropy,
service, and politics.
When Nancy Galbraith
Flinn died on April 22,
1927, she was interred
next to her husband in
the family's mausoleum
in The Homewood
Cemetery in Pittsburgh.

FAMILY FOUNDATIONS. As the patriarch of the Flinn family, William Flinn was considered quite multifaceted. In the latter part of the 1800s, Flinn partnered with James J. Booth to form what would eventually be known as the Booth and Flinn Company. The partnership was a lucrative one, with the firm being awarded numerous contracts for bridges and construction projects throughout the city of Pittsburgh and beyond.

By the Seashore. Just a few months before the end of the Civil War, Anna Oden Hagerty was born in Columbus, Ohio. She was one of several children and eventually married Henry J. Lawrence in 1885. Although they married in Ohio, according to the 1900 census, the couple was shown as living in the 20th ward of Pittsburgh, Pennsylvania. The same census enumerates their son, John Wheeler Lawrence, then nine years of age. These were the auspicious beginnings of John Wheeler Lawrence, who eventually married Mary Flinn of another prominent Pittsburgh family in 1914. John's mother, Anna Hagerty Lawrence, is shown here later in her life in a picturesque moment during a seaside retreat.

FAMILY MATTERS. The Lawrence family originally lived in Bryn Mawr, Pennsylvania, although the boys attended Shady Side Academy in Pittsburgh for their schooling. The stories of the Flinn and Lawrence families were intertwined from the early part of the 20th century. A *Pittsburgh Daily Post* article from December 31, 1909, noted that the Flinns threw a debutante party for daughter Edith, with both John Wheeler and his brother Harry Lawrence (pictured here) in attendance.

Ralph Mineart
232 Fifth Ave. Pittsburg

WHAT'S IN A NAME. This strikingly composed formal portrait of John and Harry's mother, Anna Lawrence, was taken during her younger years. This photograph can be dated using several clues identifying the time frame in which it was taken. The notation of "Ralph Mineart Studios" at "232 Fifth Avenue Pittsburg" provides the location of the portrait photographer. An entry in the *Pittsburg Press* newspaper on May 10, 1896, indicates that the studio first opened during that week. Furthermore, the unique spelling of "Pittsburg"—without its traditional "H"—indicates that the image was captured from 1891 to 1911. During that time, a nationwide postal standardization effort was underway, which resulted in the city officially dropping the last letter of its name. In these contexts, this photograph can be dated between 1896 and 1911, when Anna would have been between 7 and 22 years old. Given her appearance in the image, this was likely taken in Anna's late-teen years and dates roughly to between 1896 and 1911.

A WELL-TRAVELED WOMAN. A frequent competitor in equestrian circles at Hartwood Acres, Edith Flinn Patterson is seen here in a much more formal portrait from the estate's archival collection. Edith's hat and traveling dress are fine examples of the Edwardian fashions of the era, as showcased in this image that dates to approximately 1915. Dresses such as this were light and could be easily packed to accompany the wearer on numerous travels.

A Day at the Park. Much as we do today, a favorite pastime for people in the Edwardian era was to enjoy the benefits and landscapes of their local parks. Even while dressed in their finest attire, they would partake in such activities as a light walk, a game of tennis, or as pictured here, an afternoon on the lake in a rowboat. While the photographer and locale of this photograph are unknown, Edith Flinn gazes on with a slight smile. She is dressed head to toe in a white gown complete with gloves and a large decorative hat, the perfect picture of grace on what was assuredly a lovely afternoon.

A Beautiful Baby Boy. In this strikingly intimate portrait, new mother Edith Flinn Patterson (Mary's sister) is shown holding her infant son George Reese Patterson. The child was born on April 25, 1925. Just over a decade later in 1937, his father and Edith's husband, Simon Truby Patterson, passed away at the age of 51. Edith followed in 1961. When George Reese Patterson eventually passed in 1973, he was commemorated with a simple marker in the family mausoleum at Pittsburgh's Homewood Cemetery noting his name, dates, and the phrase "Chez Soi," meaning "at rest" or "at home."

CLARA LOUISE NEGLEY FLINN. In 1900, Clara Louise Negley married Mary's brother George Hamilton Flinn under the soaring arches and stained glass windows of Shadyside Presbyterian Church. In this archival image, Clara is shown in her wedding gown, seated for a formal portrait. The official marriage record for the couple was issued on April 18, 1900, and notes a marriage date just a few days later on April 26, 1900. Both from prominent Pittsburgh families, they would go on to have a family of their own, including daughter Louise and sons George Jr. and Lawrence.

A WALK BY THE SEA. This photograph from the Lawrence family's archives shows the boardwalk in Atlantic City, New Jersey, and dates to 1910. Travel was an important part of the lives of the family, both growing up as children and with their own families as adults. Scattered throughout the Hartwood Acres archives are a myriad of images showing vacations to the shore, mountains, and even on the bow of ships heading toward destinations unknown. In this image, the large domed building that can be seen in the background is Atlantic City's Marlborough-Blenheim Hotel; the construction of which was overseen by Thomas Edison. These buildings sat along the historic Steel Pier, which continues to operate to this day.

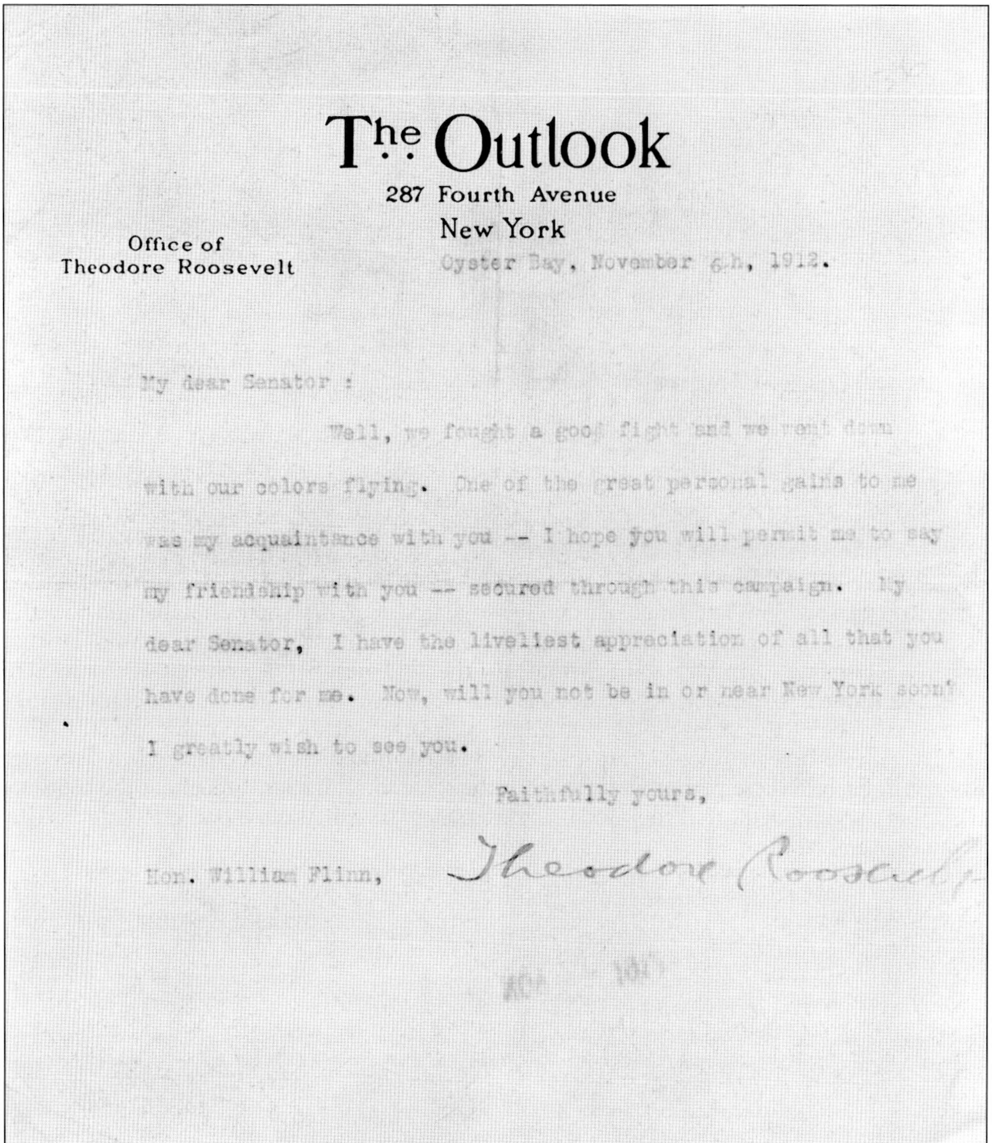

The Outlook

287 Fourth Avenue
New York

Office of
Theodore Roosevelt

Oyster Bay, November 6th, 1912.

My dear Senator :

Well, we fought a good fight and we went down
with our colors flying. One of the great personal gains to me
was my acquaintance with you -- I hope you will permit me to say
my friendship with you -- secured through this campaign. My
dear Senator, I have the liveliest appreciation of all that you
have done for me. Now, will you not be in or near New York soon?
I greatly wish to see you.

Faithfully yours,

Theodore Roosevelt

Hon. William Flinn,

FAITHFULLY YOURS. On November 5, 1912, the United States held a presidential election between candidates Woodrow Wilson (Democratic Party) and Theodore Roosevelt (Progressive Party). Wilson was declared the winner, and the following day, on November 6, 1912, Theodore Roosevelt sat down to pen this personal note to his good friend Sen. William Flinn, detailing his feelings about the outcome of the election. "We fought a good fight, and we went down with our colors flying," Roosevelt wrote. He continued to remark upon his friendship with Flinn, saying that it was one of the "great personal gains" of the campaign. The two remained friends and confidants throughout the remainder of their lifetimes.

DEEP ROOTS. The Flinn and Lawrence families were known to have many notable and powerful friends. Among them was Gifford Pinchot (pictured here at left with his brother Amos Pinchot and in a press photo with Mary), the first head of the US Forest Service when it was founded in 1905. He also held the distinction of serving as the 28th governor of the state of Pennsylvania. The roots of their friendships ran deep, and it is likely that Pinchot's relationship with the Flinn and Lawrence families developed from their close mutual affiliations with US president Theodore Roosevelt. Each of these parties moved within the same social circles throughout the course of their lifetimes and dedicated their focus toward concentrated conservation efforts protecting various natural landscapes.

A DAY AT THE "BEECH." While an exact date for this image is not known, it is similar in nature and scope to others from the Flinn family photographs that depict Beechwood Farms. The manor was acquired by family patriarch William Flinn in 1903, and this photograph likely dates to shortly thereafter as Mary Flinn is pictured here in her younger years. Her bathing suit is emblematic of the style worn during the first decade of the new century and may have even been worn as a lark, as the swimming pool behind her appears to still be under construction at the time the image was taken.

FAMILY TIES. The matriarch of the Flinn family, Nancy, had very close familial ties before she ever became a wife or mother. Born in 1851 to an Irish father and a Scottish mother, Nancy shared a sibling bond that was closer than most—she was a twin. The twin sisters, Elvira and Nancy, remained close throughout their lifetimes and are pictured here in their later years during a picturesque family get-together. Nancy is shown at right in both of these charming images from the family photograph collection.

Ralph C. Flinn
1st. Lt. 2M6N1.
A.P.O. 731.

Mr John Lawrence
c/o Mr William Flinn,
N. Hiland Ave.,
Pittsburgh,
Pa.
W. J. A

O. K.
Ralph C. Flinn
1st. Lt. 2M6N1.

A.P.O. 731, July 10, 1918.

Dear Mary, Have written all the news
to mother and father that I may tell.
You will have seen the letters by now
telling about how near Arth and I are
and what a fine Sunday we had together.
He has moved, but still will only
be twelve miles from here so I shall
see him often, isn't that fine? I have never
seen him so fine as he is right now. As
for me I am feeling fine and have

Dear Mary—Part One. The Flinn siblings were close and stayed in touch often. While away in military service, Ralph wrote this letter to his sister Mary sharing news on another of their siblings, (William) Arthur. In his own touching words, he writes, "You will have seen the letters by now telling about how near Arth and I are, and what a fine Sunday we had together. He has moved but still will only be twelve miles from here and I shall see him often. Isn't that fine? I have never seen him so fine as he is right now." The brothers remained close, with both surviving their wartime service.

Ralph E. Flinn
1st. Lt. 2M6N4.
A. P. O. 731.

Mr. John Lawrence
c/o Mr. William Flinn,
N. Hiland Ave.,
Pittsburgh,
Pa.
U. S. A.

O. K.
Ralph E. Flinn
1st. Lt. 2M6N4.

a busy and fine job under Bob Wray who
has been kindness itself to me. Was at the
front for some time and while not in great
danger I saw a lot which I may not tell.
I want you to know that I appreciate
your writing so often and that I am always
glad to get your letters they are so newsy
and Arth. feels the same about his.
My best to John and tell him I am
sorry he could not make it for I know
he must have been disappointed.
Ralph E. Flinn   Your loving brother,
1st. Lt. 2M6N4.   Ralph.
A. P. O. 731.

DEAR MARY—PART TWO. Ralph also wrote to his sister Mary about the atrocities of war. His letter to her in July 1918 said much with few words: "Was at the front for some time and while not in great danger, I saw a lot which I may not tell. I want you to know that I appreciate you writing so often."

RALPH EMERSON FLINN. Mary's older brother Ralph Emerson Flinn was the second-born of the Flinn children. Various documentation lists his birth between 1878 (per his World War I veterans service and compensation file) and 1879 (per his death certificate). As he grew older, young Ralph Flinn found employment at his father's company of Booth and Flinn, in addition to dedicating himself to military service.

SERVING WITH HONOR. Military records exist for Ralph Emerson Flinn for both World War I and World War II. His World War I veterans service and compensation file notes that Ralph served at Camp Dix in New Jersey, Camp Holabird in Maryland, Ft. Oglethorpe in Georgia, and Camp Merritt in New Jersey. Additionally, Ralph served abroad in France from January 1918 through February 1919, when he was honorably discharged.

STANLEY CHARLES PROSTREDNIK

Stanley Charles Prostrednik was born in 1901 in Nové Město n. Metuji, Czechoslovakia, the youngest of 13 children. After an apprenticeship in horticulture at the Jiran Greenhouses in Pardubice, he assisted the head horticulturist at Hradčany Castle in Prague, preparing floral decorations for President Thomas Masaryk. He served in the Czechoslovak Army (1921-1925).

From 1932-39, he was with the Civil Defense Corps and assisted many compatriots to escape through the underground. In 1939, he was arrested and imprisoned in several concentration camps. He escaped, joined the Czechoslovak Army in Exile, and fought in the Loire Valley. After the fall of France, he fled to Bermuda where he met with Jan Masaryk, en route to Washington for a meeting with Franklin D. Roosevelt.

After his arrival in the United States, he worked as a machinist and recounted his war experiences to many Czechoslovak groups. He also had a reunion with President Eduard Beneš whom he knew in Prague as Secretary of State. In 1945 he moved to Pittsburgh, and, in 1947, he became horticulturist at Hartwood, Mary Flinn Lawrence's estate.

He held offices in the Sokols and was Treasurer of the Czechoslovak Room Committee from 1957 until his death. He was a member of the Nationality Council. In 1977, he and his late wife, Anne, endowed the Stanley Prostrednik Award, an annual scholarship which enables a graduate student at the University to study abroad during the summer. He collected for Hillman Library almost 5,000 books on Czechoslovakia—many of them rare editions. His autobiography, Long Journey: Memoirs of a Czechoslovak Patriot, awaits publication.

—Margaret Mary Vojtko

MEMORIAL SERVICE

For

STANLEY PROSTREDNIK

September 16, 1986

Heinz Memorial Chapel
University of Pittsburgh

STANLEY'S STORY. On September 16, 1986, Hartwood lost one of its long-tenured and beloved caretakers. Stanley Prostrednik devoted his loving time and care to tend the finest details of the gardens of the estate. From humble beginnings in Czechoslovakia, Prostrednik worked his way up to eventually handle the arrangements at Hradcany (Prague) Castle for Czech president Thomas Masaryk. He also served in the Czech military and was a survivor of World War II prison camps, from which he escaped. That same war brought him to the United States. In 1947, while living in Pittsburgh, Prostrednik began service of a new kind—as a horticulturist at the home then known simply as "Hartwood."

On Life

"The kind of call you make in the woods is the kind of echo you will receive."

On Work

"There is a great deal of difference in working for people who know their profession and trade and who care about their work, and in working for people who do not."

On Nature

"You take out and you return."

"I follow the Laws of Nature. . .Many things, after all, are not written in any horticulture books. One has to learn by observing Nature which is an open book."

On Gardening

"Whether dealing with plants or with people, honesty is the best policy."

On Freedom

"I bled on the front for your freedom."

"If you want freedom, you must be willing to fight for it."

From **Long Journey** by Stanley Prostrednik

ORDER OF SERVICE

Organ Prelude	Dr. Don O. Franklin
Scripture Readings Corinthians I:15 Song of Songs Varia	The Reverend Bernard M. Harčariᵏ
Tribute	Dr. Edward E. Bozik
Tribute	John Lawrence
Vocal Selection	Georgia Drobny Marjorie Juba Marian Paterek
Tribute	James W. Knox
Tribute	Rackell D. Bess
Remarks	E. Maxine Bruhns
Hymn No. 218	Congregation
"A Mighty Fortress is Our God"	
Benediction	The Reverend Bernard M. Harčari
Organ Recessional	Dr. Don O. Frankli
"For All The Saints Who From Their Labors Rest" Ralph Vaughan Williams	

A LEGACY LEFT BEHIND. Stanley Prostrednik gave the gift not only of his talent and time but also the gift of knowledge. The Hillman Library at the University of Pittsburgh was the recipient of a gift from Prostrednik of over 5,000 volumes of literature pertaining to Prostrednik's home country of Czechoslovakia. Stanley Prostrednik and his wife, Anne, also endowed a scholarship that encouraged and enabled students at the university to travel to other countries for study. Upon Stanley's death in 1986, this commemorative program summarized the finer details of a long life lived in loving service and dedication to others.

WORLDS AWAY. Shown here on the war-torn fields of Germany during World War II, Lawrence Flinn (son of Mary's brother George Hamilton Flinn and his wife, Clara Louise Negley Flinn) was a staff sergeant with the 101st Infantry 26th Division of General Patton's Third Army. It was worlds away from the University of North Carolina, where he had been a philosophy professor prior to joining the military in 1943. During the Battle of the Bulge/Ardennes counteroffensive of December 1944–January 1945, Lawrence Flinn was wounded by shrapnel and was subsequently awarded the Purple Heart. In a place devastated by war, where every day was a gift, Lawrence had no idea that time was running out. On March 18, 1945, he was killed by enemy sniper fire while scouting the landscape near Hahn, Germany. For his sacrifice, Lawrence Flinn was posthumously honored with the Bronze Star Medal For Heroic Achievement and the Oak Star Cluster. Both were presented to his widow, Marion Flinn, in a service at St. Luke's Episcopal Church in East Hampton, New York, in October of 1945. Alongside Marion that day, the couple's three sons—George, Lawrence Jr., and Michael—who were all under the age of 10, would never see their father again.

S/SGT. LAWRENCE FLINN, 34854733,
Headquarters Co., 2nd Bn., 101st Inf.,
APO 26, c/o Postmaster, New York.

Saturday
December 29, 1944.

Marion Darling:

Yesterday afternoon I was just walking into a
village when the Germans started pouring their best artillery in.
One shell lit about 30 yards away around a corner, and as I was heading for the protection of the stone wall of a shed used for a wagon,
another hit about five yards away. The concussion was terrific -
my helmet went one way and I found myself lying on the cobblestone
with blood pouring off my face. I was stunned but had enough sense
to immediately crawl into the shed which was extremely lucky, for
four more shells hit right where I had been within the next thirty
seconds.

I immediately got my first-aid packet out and put
it over my cheek as I lay huddled up against the wall - strangely
enough I didn't pray or curse, but just lay there wondering if a
shell would get me. It was no fun to have pieces of tile from the
tile shingles, pieces of wood, stone and rubble come down on me. In
about ten minutes during a lull in the shelling, I managed to get back
into a house where a buddy and several other soldiers were. Fortunately
there was also a medic there who put on a clean compress. All we could
do was huddle there as the Germans followed up their barrage with a
counterattack. Fortunately we managed to beat it off, so when it
quieted down an hour later, another soldier who had a wound in the neck
and I walked back about a mile from where I had started. Before taking
off for the Aid Station, I was lucky enough to get hold of my pack
which I stripped of my G.I. stuff, so here I am with my toilet kit and
writing kit - which makes me extremely lucky as well as unusual, for
most soldiers just have the clothes (and not all of them) that they
had on their backs.

My nerves were pretty much on edge yesterday, but
it is wonderful what a night's sleep will do (especially when I hadn't
had one for three nights).

This morning I went up to the operating room and a
very nice doctor dressed my wound. It seems as though one piece of
a shell went through my cheek and lodged in the back of my throat
where my right tonsil was. So now I feel as though I had just had my
tonsil out. Another little piece is lodged just above my molar, but
the doctor said it wouldn't do any harm and just left it in. He gave
me novacain so I didn't feel a thing when he was fixing me up, but he
seemed to know his business. The doctor was from Rome, N.Y. He put
in some stitches, but said that it would not leave much of a scar.
It is on my right cheek and only about an inch long, so it will balance
the scar on my chin on the left side.

MARION DARLING. In December 1944, S.Sgt. Lawrence Flinn wrote to his beloved wife, Marion, about the hardships of World War II. In his own words, he imparted, "Yesterday afternoon, I was just walking into a village when the Germans started pouring their best artillery in. One shell lit about 30 yards away around a corner, and as I was heading for the protection of the stone wall of a shed used for a wagon, another hit about five yards away. The concussion was terrific—my helmet went one way and I found myself lying on the cobblestone with blood pouring off my face. I was stunned but had enough sense to immediately crawl into the shed which was extremely lucky, for four more shells hit right where I had been within the next thirty seconds." He enlisted on November 27, 1943, approximately a year before he wrote this letter to his wife, Marion. At the time he enlisted, he lived in Suffolk County, New York. Despite his postgraduate education, he felt the call to serve his country and left his professional occupation as a lecturer at the University of North Carolina, Duke University, and the University of Freiburg behind to join the war effort.

OFFICE OF THE CHAPLAIN
101st Infantry Regt.
APO 26

CZECHOSLOVAKIA
2 June 1945.

Mrs. Lawrence Flinn,
East Hampton,
N. Y.

Dear Mrs. Flinn:

The War Department must have informed you now that your husband has been killed in action. I shall try to give you all the information that I have about him.

Your husband, S/Sgt. Lawrence Flinn, 34854733 Hq. Co., 2nd Bn., 101st Infantry Regiment, was killed in action 18 March 1945 near Hahn, Germany. The reason why you have not received this information before is because his body could not again be found. It was to be picked up by the Graves Registration Officer but when he arrived he could not find the body. As to his death there was no doubt as various affidavits testify.

This is how it took place. Your husband went to a certain house to get better observation of the enemy's position and to locate their position for artillery concentration. He went to the attic of the house and from there he was able to direct the fire. The forward elements of the Bn. were receiving moderate small arms fire upon entering the town. They could not safely proceed until this fire was eliminated. Thus from his position he was able to direct the artillery fire upon the enemy. In this he was successful but he must have been spotted by the enemy and the result was that he was hit by a German rifle and killed. The bullet hit him in the neck.

Here is what his buddies said about him. "S/Sgt. Flinn was a most courageous soldier, always willing to undertake the most difficult and dangerous missions under most hazardous and unusual combat conditions. He won the respect and admiration of all those with whom he came in contact in his own company and the Bn."

He was also very faithful in the attendance to the services. We thus all miss him very much but it was only through the service and sacrifice of such great men that we were able to win the victory.

May I extend to you my deepest sympathy in the loss of such a wonderful husband. May God give you strength to bravely carry on even though your sorrow and grief may be heavy.

Sincerely,

(Sgd.)   PETER HONDERD

Chaplain, USA

DEAR MRS. FLINN. Six months after the aforementioned letter to Marion Flinn, heavy footfalls fell on the cobblestones as another letter was delivered into her hands. "Dear Mrs. Flinn," it began. "Your husband, S/Sgt. Lawrence Flinn . . . was killed in action 18 March 1945 near Hahn, Germany." In an attempt to better survey their position, Lawrence had climbed into the attic of a house and directed artillery fire against the enemy. In the process, however, he was spotted and felled by German sniper rifle fire. Upon his death, his friends said he "was a most courageous soldier, always willing to undertake the most difficult and dangerous missions under most hazardous and unusual combat conditions. He won the respect and admiration of all those with whom he came in contact in his own company and the Battalion." Today, a memorial stands in the Lorraine American Cemetery and Memorial in Sant-Avold, Departement de la Moselle, Lorraine, France, and much closer to his native Pittsburgh at the Homewood Cemetery.

WAR DEPARTMENT
The Adjutant General's Office
Washington 25, D. C.

In reply refer to:
AGPD-R 201 Flinn, Lawrence
34 854 733

15 August 1945

Mrs. Marion D. Flinn
Lily Pond Lane
East Hampton, New York

Dear Mrs. Flinn:

I have the honor to inform you that, by direction of the President, the Bronze Star Medal and one Oak-leaf Cluster, indicating an additional award of the Bronze Star Medal, have been posthumously awarded to your husband, Staff Sergeant Lawrence Flinn, Infantry. The citations are as follows:

BRONZE STAR MEDAL

"For heroic achievement in connection with military operations against an armed enemy near ***, Luxembourg, on 29 December 1944. During operations near ***, Staff Sergeant Flinn, headquarters Company Intelligence Sergeant, on his own initiative moved forward with the leading elements of the attacking echelon in order to set up an advanced observation post in the town. Despite being wounded by the initial barrage of hostile artillery fire and weakened by loss of blood he exposed himself to continuous artillery, mortar and small arms fire to locate a suitable Battalion Observation Post. After he had gained the necessary information and had taken part in repulsing an enemy counter-attack, he assisted another wounded soldier back to the Battalion Forward Command Post. Only when he had given the S-2 the entire situation did Staff Sergeant Flinn permit himself to be evacuated. His courage under fire, strong initiative and loyal devotion to duty reflect the highest credit upon Staff Sergeant Flinn and the armed forces of the United States."

OAK LEAF CLUSTER TO THE BRONZE STAR MEDAL

"For heroic achievement in connection with military operations against an armed enemy in Huttig-Rassweiler, Germany, on 18 March 1945. On 18 March, 1945, as the Battalion Commander of the Second Battalion and his party entered the town of Huttig-Rassweiler, they came under harassing enemy small arms fire which temporarily halted them. In order to locate the hostile positions for the direction of friendly mortar fire,

POSTHUMOUS HONORS. World War II took many husbands from many wives. At times, a posthumous effort such as the one detailed in this letter from the War Department in Washington, DC helped to soften the magnitude of the loss. When S.Sgt. Lawrence Flinn was killed in action on March 18, 1945, he earned both the Bronze Star Medal and the Oak Leaf Cluster. In August 1945, this letter was received by his widow, Marion, informing her of the designation of the honors.

FROM THE CRADLE TO THE GRAVE. The Flinn and Lawrence families spent many days together throughout their lives. Although there were several siblings, each remained close in the course of their personal, professional, and philanthropic pursuits. As they had done in life, they remained close in death, with many of the family members sharing their final resting place at the Homewood Cemetery in Pittsburgh's East End. While the name of family patriarch William Flinn is inscribed over the door, many of the Flinn relatives are interred within the family's mausoleum. These include family matriarch Nancy Galbraith Flinn, Mary and John Lawrence, Alexander Rex Flinn, Jessie Gillespie Flinn, Ralph Flinn, and William Arthur Flinn. The family portrait shown here was taken shortly before the death of family patriarch Sen. William Flinn and includes, from left to right, (first row) Mary Flinn Lawrence, Nancy Galbraith Flinn, Sen. William Flinn, and A. Rex Flinn; (second row) George Flinn, Arthur Flinn, Edith Flinn Patterson, and Ralph Flinn.

Four

STORIED STONES

Of the thousands who visit Hartwood Acres each year, there are those who come to learn of its history and those who come to enjoy its surroundings. The home, stables, and miles of trails are all a crucial part of the grounds. They share a symbiotic relationship, with aspects of one supporting multiple facets of another. The wooded trails that wind through the forests lead to the stables that were such an integral part of the Lawrence family's lives. Just up the hill from the stables, fields of flowers blossom in the summer sun throughout the carefully planned English gardens. And hidden there among the storied stones of the mansion itself rests architect Alfred Hopkins' muse—a delight for all who come across it. Hopkins's talent and vision, coupled with the boundless dedication of so many who cared for Hartwood both then and now, have made this a premier attraction in the Allegheny County parks system.

A Step Back in Time. Walking through a doorway at Hartwood is like stepping back in time. Just as so many do to this day, Mary Flinn Lawrence once walked the grounds of the estate gathering wildflowers, enjoying time with her sons, and pausing for a photograph to remember the simple quiet of a peaceful afternoon. For nearly a century, Hartwood has provided shared moments such as these, which resonate throughout the years. Many still gather and pose in front of the very doorway shown here to this day, much as Mary did in this photograph with her young son Johnny so many years ago.

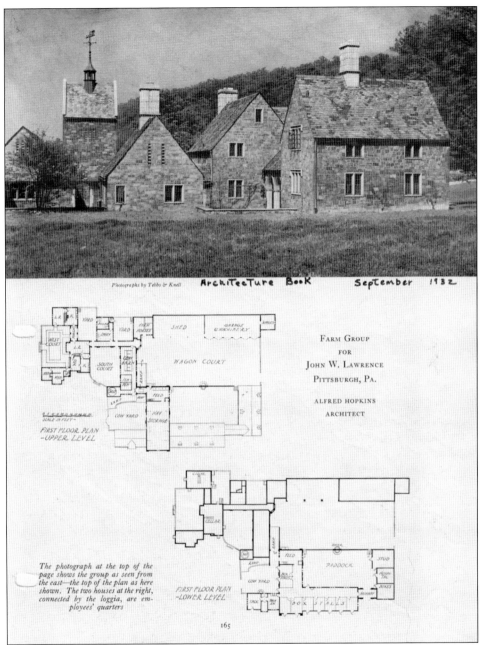

Photographs by Tebbs & Knell

ArchiTecTure Book   SepTember 1932

FARM GROUP
FOR
JOHN W. LAWRENCE
PITTSBURGH, PA.

ALFRED HOPKINS
ARCHITECT

FIRST FLOOR PLAN
–UPPER LEVEL

The photograph at the top of the page shows the group as seen from the east—the top of the plan as here shown. The two houses at the right, connected by the loggia, are employees' quarters

FIRST FLOOR PLAN
–LOWER LEVEL

165

HAND-DRAWN HISTORY. This image, dating to September 1932, presents a unique view of both the inside and outside of the stable complex. The detailed drawing denotes the cow yard, hay storage, and wagon court that were essential functions of the stables. The box stalls and tack room are also clearly noted. Caretakers lived in the two structures on the right of the image, tending the utmost care to the Lawrence family's horses. This image is credited to Tebbs & Knell, who were established architectural photographers of the day. Together, the two photographers documented locations like Chicago's Merchandise Mart and New York's Grand Central Station. As their partnership dissolved in the early 1930s, it is possible to date this photograph to the very early days of the homestead, which was built at the end of the 1920s.

HOPKINS'S MUSE. Alfred Harral Hopkins was born in 1870. The turn of the century found the young architect doing work for the well-known Vanderbilt family in Hyde Park, New York. Hopkins's work focused on farm architecture, and by 1913, he had established Alfred Hopkins & Associates on New York's fashionable Park Avenue. His success grew, and Hopkins found himself working on commissions for notables such as Louis Comfort Tiffany. During this time, Hopkins also published several works on his skill, which furthered his renown. In 1929, Hopkins was chosen by John and Mary Flinn Lawrence to design their home, Hartwood, in the style of an English country estate. Per Mary's request, the home was designed to be centrally focused around the ornate wooden paneling in the Great Hall. This paneling originally dates to the 1600s from Lee Hall castle in England and was specifically brought to the United States as a focal point for the Lawrences' new estate. As he was designing Hartwood, Hopkins whimsically featured the character seen here in the stonework just outside of the Great Hall. Today, it is known simply as "Hopkins' Muse." Other fine details also adorned the house, such as this coat of arms displayed above one of the home's entrances.

A History of Hopkins. In addition to building country estates such as Hartwood, architect Alfred Harral Hopkins was also a writer and a renaissance man. In 1902, Hopkins contributed to *Stables and Farm Buildings: A Special Number of the Architectural Review.* In 1913, he published *Modern Farm Buildings: Being suggestions for the most approved ways of designing the cow barn, dairy, horse barn, hay barn, sheepcote, piggery, manure pit, chicken house, root cellar, ice house, and other buildings of the farm group, on practical, sanitary and artistic lines,* wherein he detailed his extensive use of 16th-century architectural elements in his 20th-century designs. The book was used not only to educate the public on various architectural styles but also to assist Hopkins in soliciting clientele for future design projects.

FORM AND FUNCTIONALITY. The arched doorways, slanted roofing, and rows of windows integrated into Hopkins's architecture served measures of both form and functionality for the estates he designed. Hopkins created complexes such as the Hartwood stables shown here to be practical for horses but also suitable as living quarters for their caretakers. The balance of these facets made Hopkins's work much sought after and was one of the hallmarks of his technique.

WELCOMING COMMITTEE. When guests came to visit, they knew well to take special note of these two charming peacock sculptures that were placed just outside of the door to the family home. If the family was up to receiving company, the sculptures were positioned just as shown in this undated photograph. If, however, the family was not receiving guests that day, the birds would be turned the other way to show the back of the sculptures, and guests would know to return another day for their visit.

HELPING HANDS. The work of maintaining the Lawrences' sprawling acreage required the help of many hands. The hay that was harvested to feed the numerous horses on the estate was grown and gathered directly on the grounds. Heavy equipment and machinery helped but so did the many hands that often took part in the work. Pictured here are several of those individuals, including a young Johnny Lawrence at far right, fully immersed in the task at hand.

THE ENGLISH GARDEN AT HARTWOOD MANSION. A project by landscape architects Rose Greely and Ezra C. Stiles, the English garden at Hartwood Mansion is a timeless meditation on the harmony between nature and intentional design. Created in the 1930s shortly after the house was built, the garden is located just outside of the "cottage" area of the home (pictured in the background of this image), which was the first portion of the residence to be completed during its construction. While certainly a significant feature at the time, the gardens have retained their thoughtful creative intention and, in 2012, were recognized for their merit with inclusion in the Smithsonian's Archives of American Gardens. Mary Flinn Lawrence, a member of the Garden Club of Allegheny County, did not live long enough to see this historic designation but would undoubtedly have been honored by the touching tribute to the beloved English garden just outside her doorstep.

ROSE GREELY. Along with landscape architect Ezra C. Stiles, Rose Greely was responsible for the implementation and design of the quaint English garden which lies just outside the doors of the Hartwood Mansion. Born in February 1887, Greely made her society debut in New York in 1905. After several years of study and with a few notable projects to her credit, she became the first licensed female architect to practice in Washington, DC, in 1925. Greely's commission to design the formal English garden at Hartwood Mansion became one of the first of her lengthy career. Noting Mary Flinn's efforts to recognize the rising roles of women at this time, it is significant that she selected another prominent and pioneering woman to complete this lasting and remarkable feat of landscape design.

Ezra C. Stiles. Along with Rose Greely, Ezra C. Stiles codesigned the formal English garden at Hartwood Mansion. Descended from a president of Yale University, he was born in 1891 and received his degree in forestry and landscape architecture from Penn State in 1914. For much of the remainder of his life, he focused his efforts on various projects throughout Pittsburgh, Pennsylvania. Initially working for landscape design firm A.W. Smith, Stiles rose to prominence and opened his own firm in 1926. He was selected by many of Pittsburgh's elite families (including the Lawrences) to design portions of the grounds on their elaborate estates. Stiles's designs can also be seen in the Renziehausen Park Rose Garden and Arboretum located just outside of Pittsburgh in McKeesport, Pennsylvania.

CHRISTMAS TIME AT HARTWOOD. Accented by the striking vaulted stained-glass windows and a 1901 Steinway grand piano, a tiny Christmas tree hangs just inside one of the entrances to the Hartwood Acres mansion. Christmas decorations like this are lovingly arranged by the dedicated staff of volunteers each holiday season and enjoyed by thousands of visitors during this special time at the mansion. The piano itself was a gift given to Mary Flinn by her father, Sen. William Flinn, on the occasion of her 15th birthday. It held a prominent place in her home for the remainder of her life.

CHRISTMAS IN THE GREAT HALL. The crowning jewel of Christmas at the Hartwood Mansion is often the ornate tree that graces its ceremonious place in front of the magnificent bay of stained glass windows in the home's Great Hall. The room, which at one time hosted society balls and philanthropic events, continues to be a central focal point of the home today and is featured for tours, teas, and a myriad of other functions and gatherings throughout the year. Christmas trees were placed throughout the home for the holidays, including the home's library (below), where the family spent much of their time.

AROUND THE TABLE. The Flinn family home was host to countless social events, family dinners, and visits from various members of the social elite. Many of these took place around a table filled with the finest China, food, and laughter. Behind the scenes, the household staff worked diligently to ensure that everything went off without a hitch. Installed at the time the house was being built in the late 1920s and early 1930s, this stove (which still remains in the kitchen of the home) served as the workhorse for many of these meals and social events throughout the years.

THE GREAT CRASH OF 1929. Daily tours are one of the highlights of the 1929 mansion at Hartwood Acres and are enjoyed by both the docents who guide them and the guests who come to visit. It was during such a visit in August of 2005 when a tour passed through the Great Hall, with the docent noting the details of the four-centuries-old wooden paneling and intricately detailed molded plaster ceiling. Just a few minutes later, as the tour continued upstairs, a loud crash was heard as a singular two-ton piece of that ceiling came crashing to the floor. Craftsmen from the Western Pennsylvania Craftsmen Guild, including plasterer Daniel McClelland, worked to complete the ceiling repairs in conjunction with woodworking repairs done by George Starz. Both men were meticulous in their efforts, ensuring accuracy down to fractions of an inch and carefully laboring to ensure historically accurate restorations. The repairs took nearly seven months (during which the mansion was closed) and cost nearly $300,000 at the time. Once completed, it was a testament to the skill of the craftsmen that the restored portion was once again indistinguishable from the original workmanship.

A Restful Retreat. Far away from the halls of the house which hosted social gatherings and family events, John and Mary Flinn Lawrence's upstairs bedrooms and dressing rooms served as a quiet respite from the rest of the home. Mary's dressing room featured paneling accented by a row of tall gleaming windows that let the natural light stream in to fill up the room. A marble and wood-carved fireplace heated the interior during cold Pennsylvania winters. Nearby, Mary's bedroom featured the ethereal adornments of hand-painted florals, vines, and delicate butterflies delicately detailed along each wall. Crystal sconces dripped luminous rainbows of light across the floor while a row of windows invited the warmth of a calming summer breeze. Most poignantly, a framed photograph of her husband, John, was featured prominently on the dresser, forever keeping him close as she drifted off to dream.

Five

EQUESTRIAN ECHOES

The footfalls of horses' hooves once fell against the sun-warmed cobblestones that graced the many paths at Hartwood. As much as the Lawrence family, these equestrian echoes are synonymous with the history of the home. To this day, visitors ride their horses throughout the wooded trees and alongside the places where competitions and social events like the fox hunt and junior championships once took place. For each of the Lawrence family members—John, Mary, Johnny, and Billy—the horses were more than simply animals that resided in the nearby stables. Along with the horses' primary caretaker, Merle "Brownie" Brown, the Lawrence family displayed a tender affection and dedicated role in nurturing the well-being of their four-legged companions. So much so that long after the others have gone, a few of the family's beloved steeds remain in a sense that is often shared with visitors to this day.

THE STABLES. As much at home in the quiet English countryside as the rolling hills of Western Pennsylvania, the stables were home to numerous horses on the estate, as well as their caretaker, Merle Brown, affectionately called "Brownie." Several of the horses charged to Brownie's care throughout the years were Donnie B, Wonder Girl, and Dunloe. Donnie B required detailed care due to both environmental and food allergies. Wonder Girl was a show horse frequently ridden during the fox hunts. Dunloe shared some of the same markings as her dam, Wonder Girl.

SLEIGH BELLS RING. While Hartwood was known to host numerous and well-attended summer equestrian events, the family also made the most of the grounds and their horses during Western Pennsylvania's blustery winter months. Mary Flinn Lawrence takes the reins here, alongside her niece Isabel Patterson and sons, Johnny and Billy Lawrence. Their horse, Blackbird, was often chosen to pull the sleds. This image was presented in the February 7, 1943, edition of the *Pittsburgh Sun-Telegram*, noting that the method of transportation was used to take son John to school in Dorseyville, as a means of conserving gasoline and tires during wartime. Sled rides were a common occurrence on the grounds, as the meandering wooded trails provided many opportunities to enjoy this winter pastime.

MADE WITH LOVE. Much beloved by the family and equestrian residents of Hartwood, Merle Brown (affectionately known as "Brownie") was part of the heart and soul of the estate for decades. After his early work at Ligonier's Rolling Rock Club, he found employment with Edith Flinn Patterson, Mary Flinn Lawrence's sister. Brownie later took over the schooling and training of Hartwood's horses as a stable hand in 1937. His relationship with the family was a close one, and the Brown family would often attend Christmas mornings with the Lawrences. It was Brownie who taught the Lawrence sons how to ride their treasured Welsh ponies, Tommy Tucker and Cinders, while always keeping a soft spot in his heart for one of his favorite horses of the estate, the Lawrences' prized thoroughbred, Donnie B. Brownie, well known for the adornments that graced the stables, including his hand-woven straw mats found alongside the stalls. Brownie also crafted wreaths such as the one pictured here, which were sold in the gift shop of the estate after it was sold to Allegheny County in 1969.

BROWNIE POINTS. Pictured in front of the stables that were home to both of them, one of the Lawrence family's exquisite horses is shown here being cared for by Merle "Brownie" Brown. At one time, the stables housed nearly 15 of the family's horses, which were used for family rides, competitions, and hunts held on the property. Brownie not only cared for the family's horses but the Lawrence boys as well, to whom he was very close. He taught them to ride from a very young age on their ponies, Cinders and Tommy Tucker. The boys were quite accomplished and won ribbons in many junior-class horse shows. Brownie himself often placed in the senior class at similar events. Also shown here, a young Johnny Lawrence rides one of the family's beloved ponies on the lawn, with the Hartwood estate in the background.

STABLE GROUNDS. Beautifully illuminated in the crepuscular rays of the late afternoon sunlight, this image shows the horse stables as they appeared during the course of Mary Flinn Lawrence's lifetime. The family's horses were kept on-site in these stables, including several of Mary's favorites. The straw mats lining the stall entryways were woven by hand, and each horse's bucket, resting outside of the stall, was accented with the family's initial, "L," wrapped in a circlet.

BROWNIE'S BUILDING. From 1937 until 1972, Merle "Brownie" Brown tended the horses at the Lawrence family's stables, shown here. Even after Hartwood was acquired by the Allegheny County Parks Department, Brownie stayed on as a caretaker and frequent guide to visitors. He often showcased the stable complex, explaining how he had expertly cared for the horses for nearly half a century. The horses were exceptionally well cared for, using hand-crafted oak feed buckets with brass accents emblazoned with intricately detailed initials.

A STABLE ENVIRONMENT. Appearing much then as it does now, the stable complex at Hartwood has remained virtually unchanged since it was originally built in the late 1920s. The stables were the first structures built on the property and completed before the formal residence had been built. Caretakers also resided here in quarters alongside the family's beloved horses.

A Stable Fixture. Horses were not only a key component of everyday activities at Hartwood, but were also integrated into many decorative aspects of the home. Adorning the wall of the courtyard just outside of the stables, the sculpture shown here served as both a decorative and useful feature of the grounds. It was placed above the watering trough within the stable complex and provided a fresh stream of water from which the family's horses would drink. It remains there to this day, although the horses it once nourished are long gone.

THE FINER DETAILS. Although the residence at Hartwood abounds with intricate features and notable characteristics, these qualities are not limited to the home alone. Just down the hill, the stable complex was also designed with a fine consideration for aspect and class. The name of this particular horse has been lost to time, but the loving care shown transcends in this photograph. The saddle is removed from the hook, but the bridle hangs nearby. Also worth noting are the beautifully handmade buckets that adorned the stables, each emblazoned with an "L" monogram, denoting the Lawrence family name.

TACK RACK. A sporting jacket and boots rest on display here alongside a stand specifically made to display and hold the riding tack that was used by the Lawrence family. Equipment such as saddles, saddle blankets, breastplates, stirrups, and reins was all commonplace throughout the barn and often neatly organized by utility stands, such as the one shown here.

SITTING SIDE SADDLE. Although her sister Mary was well-known for the equestrian events she hosted at Hartwood Acres, Edith Flinn Patterson (shown here) was also a very adept horsewoman. Edith is shown here sitting side-saddle, which likely indicates she was participating in one of the many fox hunts held on the grounds of the Hartwood Acres estate at the time. The riding habit depicted here is also indicative of traditional fox-hunting attire of the early 20th century. As Edith's homestead, Harkaway Farms, was located adjacent, she was likely in attendance at many of the major sporting events that took place on Hartwood's grounds.

HONORED TRADITIONS. Honoring a tradition going back thousands of years, Mary strictly rode side-saddle on her horses. The balance strap affixed to the back portion of the saddle helped to hold it in place on the horse as she rode. Originally, a wooden step called a planchette was used to accommodate ladies as they rode in this manner. Throughout the centuries, saddles were developed that allowed women to better control both their place on the horse and the animal as they moved. Saddles such as this were also designed to allow women to display their gowns while at the same time maintaining the safety of the rider. Certain riding habits were designed with aprons, which allowed the back of the gown to be swept to the side when riding. This was essential to preventing the women's clothing from becoming entangled in the saddle. Eventually, the design of the saddles evolved to include not one but two pommels, on which women could balance their legs while the horse would walk, trot, or canter.

WOVEN WITH LOVE. This interior view of the stables at Hartwood showcases the love, care, and dedication that Merle "Brownie" Brown showed for the horses in his charge. Made from hand, some of his finest work is on display here in the meticulously woven carpets that adorned the walkways outside of each of the horse stalls. Also showcased on the wall outside of the stalls is one of the beautiful wreaths which Brownie also wove by hand. When Hartwood Acres was first under the care of Allegheny County, Brownie often sold these mementos to visitors who would come to appreciate both the property and his fine handiwork.

HORSEPOWER. Besides the family that lived there, the horses that once lived at these stables were a driving force of the Hartwood estate. Directly behind the stable complex, a series of garages housed maintenance equipment and the family's vehicles. Shown at right in this image is a vehicle that was used for family outings beyond the expansive hillsides of their Indiana and Hampton Townships home.

OVER THE TOP. The elder Lawrences were not the only accomplished riders in the family. From a very young age, their boys Johnny and Billy were also taught how to ride. Their cousins at the adjacent home of Harkaway Farms (estate of Mary's sister Edith's family) were also active in the riding community and often participated in equestrian events held at Hartwood. Shown here, young Johnny Lawrence expertly executes a jump on one of his many trusted ponies. Competitive events often took place on the grounds, which included the estate, stables, and an equestrian ring designed to host such occasions.

TAKING A LEAP. Numerous equestrian competitions took place on the grounds at Hartwood throughout the years. These were attended by well-known Pittsburghers, as well as competitors from the area such as the Flaccus family, who lived near Hartwood. Shown here, several riders at Hartwood participate in a jumping competition. From fox hunts to horse shows, Hartwood served as one of the ultimate centers for equestrian showmanship in the Pittsburgh area from its very earliest days.

NATURE AND NURTURE. From the time John and Mary Flinn Lawrences' boys Johnny and Billy (shown below) were young, they nurtured a connection with the family's horses not only through showmanship, but almost as members of the family. Throughout the years, many animals called the estate's stables home. Each in turn would not only be cared for by members of Hartwood's staff but also by the members of the Lawrence family. Young Johnny is shown left with one of the well-cared-for animals in his charge.

COMPETITION DAY. With a look of determination on the young boy's face, Johnny Lawrence is shown here during one of the many equestrian competitions that took place at Hartwood. Following in the footsteps of their mother, Mary, both of the boys would often compete alongside their cousins and other junior competitors in various events.

Supporting the War on a Far Foreign Shore. The Lawrence family's dedication and support of military causes are well documented. On June 22, 1940, Hartwood hosted the popular Fox Chapel Junior Horse Show. Sons Johnny and Billy (pictured here) often joined in these events. The benefit was integrated with war relief efforts to support causes abroad as World War II raged throughout Europe. Proceeds from the event that day benefited the L'Union des Femmes de France and the Women's Auxiliary of the British War Relief Fund. It would be another year and a half before the United States itself was drawn into the war with the bombing of Pearl Harbor on December 7, 1941.

The Eloquent Equestrian. Mary Flinn held a lifelong love of horses. She shared an innate connection with them that measured well beyond the numerous events she competed in throughout her lifetime. Captured here in a simplistic but elegant moment, it is clear to see the kinship that was such an integral part of life at Hartwood. Throughout her lifetime, Mary cared for numerous horses at the homestead's stable complex, which is likely the location where this photograph was taken in the latter portion of Mary's life.

LIFELONG LOVE. Throughout her lifetime, Mary Flinn Lawrence (52 years old in this image) was an accomplished equestrian but also enjoyed time spent with the many horses that were a part of her home life from childhood through adulthood. While several were kept on the Hartwood Acres property, two were eventually memorialized with a place in a private horse cemetery on the grounds. Along a quiet path that leads back through the woods, nearly within view of the stables, rest two tiny grey headstones. Andra (1944–1954) and Sheila (1946–1959) are noted as having been "Faithful Unto Death" and "Loved and Loving," respectively. A quiet stone bench sits nearby, allowing those who stop to linger perhaps the same sense of solitude that Mary once felt while sitting in the same exact spot.

Six

MEMORIES AND MOMENTS

The social events held at Hartwood were opulent, entertaining, and full of moments remembered for decades. The home itself seemed made for entertaining, and lavish parties, fundraisers, and social gatherings were often hosted by the Lawrences in the Great Hall. High society soirees such as these were familiar to the couple. Their own wedding in 1914 had been meticulously detailed, and mementos of it can still be found throughout the halls of the home they shared together. In addition to the events held within Hartwood's formal gathering spaces, the grounds also played host to a number of celebrations and competitions throughout the decades. One of the best-known and well-attended events was the Fox Chapel Hunt, which perfectly integrated the rich equestrian traditions and natural landscape. At the center of it all with dignified grace, elegant poise, and quiet fortitude was Mary and the home she called Hartwood.

will please present this card at the

Sixth United Presbyterian Church

on Thursday, the eleventh of June

JUNE 11, 1914. The afternoon of Thursday, June 11, 1914, was a memorable day in the city of Pittsburgh. Members of its finest families were invited to gather together for the marriage of the eldest daughter of Sen. William and Nancy Galbraith Flinn, Mary, to John Wheeler Lawrence. The Sixth United Presbyterian Church on North Highland Avenue was to be the location for the ceremony, with access only granted upon presentation of this delicate calling card, which had been included along with the wedding invitation. This particular example from the Hartwood Acres archives is incomplete, but those that were sent would have included the bearer's name beneath the imprinted family crest.

POLISHED TO PERFECTION. This intricate Dutch silver serving set is part of the treasured collection of serving ware that remains at Hartwood and was used at numerous societal events held by Mary Flinn Lawrence at her home. A few years prior to the time that Hartwood was being built in 1929, Mary's childhood home (Braemar) was demolished. Given the proximity of the timing of the demolition of one estate, and the subsequent construction of the other, it is known that many of the accoutrements at Hartwood originated from Braemar. To further illustrate this connection, several items such as wall sconces and serving sets like these can be found in both old photographs of Braemar and are still utilized during events at Hartwood today. Many events took place in Hartwood's dining room, complete with a crystal chandelier and a formal painted portrait of Mary's father, Sen. William Flinn, sharing company with guests as they visited the Lawrence family's home.

COSTUMED CAPERS. Not all events on the grounds of Hartwood were formal. This snapshot, likely dating to the late 1930s, evokes a day full of fun and merriment. Mary is shown at left wearing a charming bohemian costume. Her husband, John, wears similar attire while gently guiding a donkey carrying a woven basket full of wildflowers. The exact nature of this event is unknown, but it exemplifies the fun family atmosphere that was at the very heart of their home.

THE HUNT. This image from the archives shows not only the ridges surrounding the estate but also one of the many hunts which took place there. While this specific event is unknown, the Fox Chapel Hunt took place on these grounds on numerous occasions. Families came from neighboring counties and would rest in the peaceful shade of the forested grounds during intermissions. Among the spectators were members of the family, including Edith Flinn Patterson, sister of Mary Flinn Lawrence. Edith's daughters Isabelle and Nancy also participated in riding during these events.

A Formal Affair. Many of the social gatherings that Mary attended centered around political or philanthropic events—and sometimes both. Mary Flinn Lawrence was well known for her fundraising efforts on behalf of women's rights, children's charities, and other causes that she held close to her heart. As such, it was not unusual for black-tie events to be a common occurrence within their social circles. While this specific occasion is not known, Mary is immediately recognizable in the front row (at right) for her composure, poise, grace, and the quiet dignity with which she carried herself.

THE HEART OF THE HOME. Throughout her lifetime, Mary Flinn Lawrence (shown here at the center, wearing white) retained her status as a society hostess. She often hosted fundraisers, such as this one in her own home. This particular soiree took place at Hartwood. Although the specific circumstances surrounding the event are not known, it likely occurred in the early 1950s based on the style of attire worn by the women in attendance. Long after her death in 1974, Mary was remembered for the love she gave her children, the kindness she showed to others, and the warm sense of generosity and philanthropy that she shared with the world.

Discover Thousands of Local History Books Featuring Millions of Vintage Images

Arcadia Publishing, the leading local history publisher in the United States, is committed to making history accessible and meaningful through publishing books that celebrate and preserve the heritage of America's people and places.

Find more books like this at
www.arcadiapublishing.com

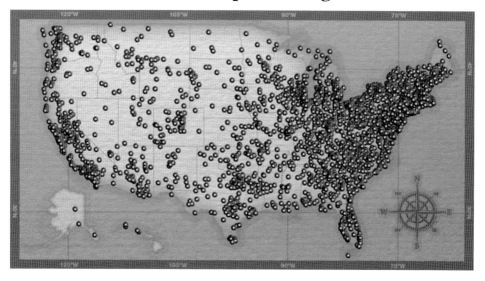

Search for your hometown history, your old stomping grounds, and even your favorite sports team.

Consistent with our mission to preserve history on a local level, this book was printed in South Carolina on American-made paper and manufactured entirely in the United States. Products carrying the accredited Forest Stewardship Council (FSC) label are printed on 100 percent FSC-certified paper.

MADE IN THE USA